Lead!

They will follow you as you follow Jesus.

Stephen D. Owens

Publisher: Alpha Lending & Investments, LLC. Owensministry@gmail.com
www. StephenOwens.org

All Scripture quotations, unless otherwise indicated, are taken from the Holy Bible, King James Version. Copyright © 1908, 1917, 1929, 1934, 1957, 1964,1982 by Thomas Nelson Inc., Used by permission. All rights reserved.

Other versions used:

ESV – Scripture quotations are from The ESV® Bible (The Holy Bible, English Standard Version®), Copyright © 2001 by Crossway, a publishing ministry of Good News Publishers. Used by permission. All rights reserved.

NLT – Scripture quotations marked NLT are taken from the Holy Bible, New Living Translation, Copyright © 1996, Used by permission by Tyndale House Publishers, Inc., Wheaton, Illinois 60189. All rights reserved.

NKJV – Scripture taken from the New King James Version. Copyright © 1982 by Thomas Nelson, Inc., Used by permission. All rights reserved.

NASB – Scripture taken from the NEW AMERICAN STANDARD BIBLE ®, Copyright © 1960, 1962, 1963, 1968, 1971, 1972, 1973, 1975, 1977, 1995 by The Lockman Foundation, Used by permission. All rights reserved.

ISBN-10: 0982462247

ISBN-13: 978-0982462249

Copyright © 2014, 2022 Stephen D. Owens

All rights reserved. No part of this book may be reproduced, stored in a retrieval system, or transmitted in any form or by any means, electronic, mechanical, photocopying, recording, or otherwise, without the prior written permission of the publisher. Further information may be obtained from Alpha Lending & Investments, LLC.

Copyright © 2022
Stephen D. Owens
All Rights Reserved

ISBN-10: 0982462247
ISBN-13: 978-0982462249

Table of Contents

☙

Introduction 7

Leading Begins With Following 9

DISCIPLINE 1: Spending Time With God 19

DISCIPLINE 2: Being Secure In Your
Leadership 27

DISCIPLINE 3: Suffering Well For Jesus 31

DISCIPLINE 4: Communication Is Essential 39

DISCIPLINE 5: Entrepreurial Visionary 51

DISCIPLINE 6: Focus On Leadership
Duplication 59

DISCIPLINE 7: Team-Base Ministry 67

DISCIPLINE 8: Don't Be Afraid To Talk
About Money 73

DISCIPLINE 9: The Goal Is To Finish 81

Leading With Proper Perspective 87

Book Recommendations 91

Biography 93

Introduction

༄

This small book is a reflection on what I have seen in Scripture and my leadership journey as a church planter. I planted a church in 2009 called Triumphant Assembly as a small Bible study inside of an YMCA (Young Men's Christian Association) building in Bedford, Ohio, USA. It was a small church plant with people who loved Jesus and other people. We wanted to impact Cleveland and its surrounding area for the Savior.

When I planted this ministry, I didn't have a core team, a sponsoring church, or any financial backing. I did, however, have God and the Bible. I also read many books on leadership and went to a few local pastors for counsel because I had a very strong desire to have a healthy biblical church that made disciples for Jesus.

I wouldn't have been considered a high-capacity leader when I wrote this book. But I had a passion for pleasing God and for reaching people for Jesus, so I was willing to learn and grow into the leader God was calling me to be within his church.

The best way I saw to develop my leadership, and the leadership of those around me was to concentrate on a few areas of leadership and continually practice getting better at them. Those areas are what this book is about. As you read, I pray you're encouraged to move forward in your leadership development.

Leading Begins With Following

☙

If a commission by an earthly king is considered an honor, how can a commission by a Heavenly King be considered a sacrifice?

- David Livingstone

If you can't follow, you can't lead. This should be the mantra of the Christian leader. Why? If you can't follow well, you will not be able to lead well. While we can learn valuable leadership skills from the experiences of people, we don't have a relationship with via books, podcasts, seminars, and documentaries. I believe one of the best ways to learn how to lead is by observing the lives, behaviors, and communication skills of leaders we are connected to in the local church. We learn what to do and hopefully what not to do.

One of the first things every Christian leader can show future leaders is that their ultimate allegiance is to King Jesus. Jesus, our Lord, and savior, is our leader, and he is the greatest example of leadership. As leaders, we must submit our leadership to his lordship because we will not be effective in the local church without him. Jesus tells us, "Follow me, and I will make you fishers of men" (Matthew 4:19). If church leaders are not following Jesus, then they are not leading for him. They are leading for themselves.

He tells us if we follow him, he will make us into people who will fish for souls for his glory. If that is one of his primary objectives for his followers, we must ask ourselves, "How do we catch people?" We can't use physical lures or nets to catch them. We have to use something else. One of the components we must use is influence. We fish for people to make them disciples of Jesus by influencing them through relationship, behavior, and conversation. The leader who can't influence people will not be a very good fishers of men. Let's look at influence for a moment.

If we want to influence people for the purpose of helping them become disciples of Jesus, we must allow them into our lives to see how we live as a follower of Jesus. We have to allow them to see how we care for our family. They need to see how we deal with pressure, frustration, and setbacks; how we pray and study the Scriptures.

When it comes to influencing future leaders, not only do we need to allow them to spend time around us in ministry settings, we must allow them to be around us outside of worship services and events so they can see the real us. That is what Jesus did with the twelve. He allowed them to see him when he wasn't preaching, teaching, and serving the crowd.

Self - denial

Jesus even told his future twelve leaders how to become great leaders like himself, which should be our goal as well – to lead like Jesus. Matthew wrote in his gospel letter, "Then Jesus said to his disciples, If anyone wishes to come after me, he must deny himself, and take up his cross and follow me" (Matthew 16:24). Jesus is telling them and us how to follow in his leadership footsteps.

The initial skill we must constantly practice is self-denial. We must deny ourselves of our sinful desires and the temptation to live self-centered lives. Leaders who follow Jesus should not be selfish and self-centered. We should be marked by humility and an ability to sacrifice for others. We should strive to help others grow, develop, and get closer to Jesus.

This act of denying ourselves is also known as carrying our cross. Cross bearing isn't pleasurable. As leaders, there will be times when we will have to suffer for Jesus. Leaders can and do get hurt leading for Jesus. They can get hurt emotionally, financially, and even physically.

The idea and image of the cross is not comfort and security but pain and death. We have to learn to die daily so others can live by meeting Jesus through his gospel. We must let future leaders and our congregations know we must bear our cross by following Jesus first and foremost.

We must also teach them while they need to follow Jesus's leadership, they must also follow the leadership in that local assembly. We must help them understand through the word of God that they are also following Jesus when they submit to the biblical leadership that God has in place in that church.

Being an Example

They need to follow those individuals God has placed there to lead the church. Not only following their guidance from the bible, but also how they live. That's what the Apostle Paul told the church in Thessalonica in his second letter to them. He writes,

"For you yourselves know how you ought to follow our example because we did not act in an undisciplined manner among you. Nor did we eat anyone's bread without paying for it, but with labor and hardship, we kept working night and day so that we would not be a burden to any of you not because we do not have the right to this, but in order to offer ourselves as a model for you, so that you would follow our example." (2 Thessalonians 3:7-9).

Let's look at these verses for a moment. In verse seven, the Apostle Paul told the church they knew how they were supposed to follow their example. This implies they already knew the pattern the apostles had put in place. Paul reminded them of the lifestyle he and his team lived while they were with them. They lived that way to show them how to live.

At the end of verse seven, he told them how he and his companions didn't live undisciplined lives among them. They wanted to set a standard, so they lived a disciplined life. The apostles' lives were stable and consistent.

Then he wrote about the standard (example) they set before them. The apostles didn't eat bread they didn't pay for. They worked jobs to get money so they wouldn't be a burden on the new church. They exemplified how believers should not be a burden on their brothers and sisters in the Lord.

They lived this way in front of the new Christians in Thessalonica because the apostles had foresight. They knew they would have to leave them one day. Therefore, they needed to set a pattern of how Christians should treat each other.

Finally, in verse nine, he reminded them how they did not ask the church to take care of them. Not because they weren't supposed to, because they would have been within their boundaries to ask for compensation seeing how they planted the church and taught them the word of God. Yet, there was something more important to the apostles than receiving compensation; they wanted to have a pattern in place for when they left.

The apostles' pattern within the church would allow those new believers to grow spiritually, love each other well, and help them be examples for future Christians. Therefore, the apostles offered themselves as models and examples for the church by putting their lives on display.

Following the examples of the apostles, leaders, we must live lives worthy of following; lives that are disciplined and not burdensome. Leaders, we have to know people are looking at our lifestyle to figure out how to follow Jesus and how to interact with other Christians.

We have to intentionally put our lives on display so people can learn how to live for Jesus. Besides, they are going to be looking at our lives anyway, so we might as well give them something to look at that will encourage them to follow Jesus.

Follow Me

A while ago, I was asked to teach a seminar on leadership, and I began to search the Scripture to find a passage that I could use as a basis for the seminar. I came across 1 Corinthians 11:1, "Be ye followers of me, even as I also am of Christ." As I meditated on this verse, I found it to be one of the most concise statements on leadership within the local church.

The more I studied the verse, the more I began to understand that the Apostle Paul wanted people to follow him. Not because he wanted glory for himself, nor was he selfish, or self-centered, or egotistical. He wanted people to follow him so he could show them how to follow Jesus.

Do you want people to follow you? Not because you want your ego stroked, or for money and status but because you can lead them to Jesus. I believe leaders should want to lead.

The Apostle Paul wanted to lead people. He even told Timothy, "if any man desire the office of a bishop, he desire a good work." He used the word "desire". A leader must have a desire to lead.

If leaders don't want to lead and don't want people to follow their leadership, then leadership probably isn't for you. The church of Jesus Christ does not need half-hearted, disgruntled, unmotivated leaders. It needs leaders who are passionate about glorifying Jesus, the word of God, loving people, and leadership.

The Apostle Paul tells the church in Corinth to follow (imitate) him as he followed (imitated) Christ. He wanted them to live like him as he lived like Jesus. He wanted them to submit to his leadership as he submitted to Jesus's leadership. He wanted them to lead like him as he led like Jesus.

The leader's life should reflect the life of Jesus. This doesn't mean we will be perfect or sinless. Only Jesus is perfect and sinless. But we should strive to live like Jesus, submit our lives to him, and pattern our leadership after him. If we are striving to be like Jesus, we should want people to follow (imitate) us because we want to show them how to live for Jesus.

1 Corinthians 11:1 sparked me to look at the life and leadership of the Apostle Paul. The rest of this book is about nine church leadership disciplines I observed examining his ministry. These nine disciplines have helped me to become a better leader within the local church.

Even though I am no longer a church planter, I'm still trying to get better at these disciplines. I believe these disciplines if practiced, will help believers lead more like Jesus. The more they practiced, the better you will become at them.

Now, I am not lifting up the Apostle Paul as the greatest leader in the Bible, because the greatest example of leadership is Jesus. The Apostle Paul is a human being just like us who had flaws and shortcomings. For example, he didn't practice the concept of mercy very well with John Mark in Acts 15:36 – 41.

He refused to give John Mark a second chance to develop his leadership ability when he refused to let him come on a second journey with him. His stubbornness caused a ministry team to split. Barnabas and Paul could not agree on allowing John Mark to accompany them on their missionary journey, so they would stop doing ministry together. Barnabas wanted to give him another chance, but Paul didn't. I believe, their ministry together split over Paul not showing mercy.

Paul eventually softened his heart and saw value in John Mark's ministry. At the end of his apostolic career, Paul wrote to Timothy and told him to bring John Mark with him when he came to visit because John Mark was "very useful" to Paul (2 Timothy 4:11,

ESV). Yet, John Mark didn't become useful for ministry through the assistance of the Apostle Paul. He became very useful through the training of Barnabas and the Apostle Peter. If you want to find out more about the life, leadership, and legacy of John Mark, read my book *The Next Leader.*

DISCIPLINE 1:
Spending Time With God

୧୨

There is no way that Christians, in a private capacity, can do so much to promote the work of God and advance the kingdom of Christ as by prayer.

- Jonathan Edwards

The first discipline we must focus on is spending time with God. This is a crucial discipline, because we can't spend all of our time doing work for the Lord and not being with the Lord of the work. As a bi-vocational church planter, I had to fight against the temptation of spending all my time outside of my occupation preparing messages and Bible studies, creating strategies, and doing ministry. I had to make sure I spent quiet time with God for my personal growth.

When we fall into this temptation, not only do we neglect to spend time with God, but we will also neglect spending time with our families. I constantly recalibrated my priorities to make sure I was spent time with God in prayer and Bible reading. When I did, it reflected in my time with my family and in my ministry.

We see the Apostle Paul practiced this discipline from the outset of his conversion. Let's take some time to read a portion of Acts chapter nine. This is after Paul, rather Saul at that time had an encounter with Jesus and got saved. Acts 9:8-18 reads,

> Saul rose from the ground, and although his eyes were opened, he saw nothing. So they led him by the hand and brought him into Damascus. And for three days, he was without sight, and neither ate nor drank.
>
> Now there was a disciple at Damascus named Ananias. The Lord said to him in a vision, "Ananias." And he said, "Here I am, Lord." And the Lord said to him, "Rise and go to the street called Straight, and at the house of Judas look for a man of Tarsus named Saul, for behold, he is praying, and he has seen in a vision a man named Ananias come in and lay his hands on him so that he might regain his sight."

But Ananias answered, "Lord, I have heard from many about this man, how much evil he has done to your saints at Jerusalem. And here he has authority from the chief priests to bind all who call on your name." But the Lord said to him, "Go, for he is a chosen instrument of mine to carry my name before the Gentiles and kings and the children of Israel. For I will show him how much he must suffer for the sake of my name."

So Ananias departed and entered the house. And laying his hands on him, he said, "Brother Saul, the Lord Jesus who appeared to you on the road by which you came has sent me so that you may regain your sight and be filled with the Holy Spirit." And immediately, something like scales fell from his eyes, and he regained his sight. Then he rose and was baptized; and taking food, he was strengthened. (ESV)

What did Jesus tell Ananias Saul (Paul) was doing at the house of Judas? He is praying. He was by himself spending time with God. Not only was he praying, but in verse nine, we see he had not eaten or had anything to drink in three days. He is also fasting during this time.

The Apostle Paul is alone with God, praying and fasting. How often do you spend time alone with

God in prayer? There is no way we can live like Jesus, submit to Jesus and lead like Jesus if we don't spend time talking to the Father like Jesus.

As we continue to look at Paul's life, we see how he prays as a leader within the church. Not only does he talk to God about himself, but he also prays for the church. He takes time while he is praying to talk to God about those who follow him. Paul writes to the church in Ephesus:

"For this reason, because I have heard of your faith in the Lord Jesus and your love toward all the saints, I do not cease to give thanks for you, remembering you in my prayers, that the God of our Lord Jesus Christ, the Father of glory, may give you the Spirit of wisdom and of revelation in the knowledge of him, having the eyes of your hearts enlightened, that you may know what is the hope to which he has called you, what are the riches of his glorious inheritance in the saints" (Ephesians 1:15-18, ESV)

He tells the Ephesians; he does not stop thanking God for them because of their faith in Jesus, and their love for other Christians. Then he asks God to give them three items: wisdom, revelation, and enlightenment. He wanted them to know the hope they had in Jesus, which was their glorious inheritance.

As a leader, when was the last time you prayed like that for those who follow you? When we pray, we have to not only pray for ourselves and our family, but we must also pray for people who aren't related to us, especially the saints. We must thank God for the spiritual growth Christians have achieved. We must ask God to give them what they need to keep growing so they can get an even better understanding of what God has given them in His Son.

A helpful format to follow in our prayer time is the Lord's Prayer in Matthew 6:9-13.

"⁹In this manner, therefore, pray: Our Father in heaven, Hallowed be Your name. ¹⁰Your kingdom come. Your will be done On earth as it is in heaven. ¹¹Give us this day our daily bread. ¹²And forgive us our debts, As we forgive our debtors. ¹³And do not lead us into temptation, But deliver us from the evil one. For Yours is the kingdom and the power and the glory forever. Amen."

To help people use the Lord's Prayer as a guide to prayer, some have used the 7 P's to give structure to prayer time.

- Praise – V.7
- Purpose – V.10
- Provision – V.11

- Pardon – V.12
- People – V.12
- Protection – V.13
- Praise – V.13

Paul not only spent time with God by himself. He also spent time with God in the company of other leaders. Do you pray with other leaders? The Apostle Paul did. Not only did he pray with other leaders. He also fasted with them.

Acts 13:3 tells us how Paul worshipped the Lord with the other leaders at the church of Antioch in prayer and fasting. Acts 16:25 tells us while Paul and Silas was in jail in the city of Thyatira, they "were praying and singing hymns to God." They had a prayer meeting in jail while they were in the midst of opposition and tribulation. We, as leaders, have to spend time together worshipping God. Leaders must pray, sing hymns and fast together as they lead for the Lord.

Included in the time Paul spent with God, he also read books. The Apostle Paul was a reader. The old cliché is still true - "leaders are readers." In the second letter Paul wrote to his young apprentice Timothy, the Apostle told him when he visits to bring with him "the books, but especially the parchments." (2 Timothy 4:13)

In this statement, there are two categories of reading material; the books, which is a general category, and the parchments. Some say the parchments were probably the Old Testament writings. If that is the case, then Paul read the Old Testament as well as other books.

The Scriptures show us that Paul placed a high value on reading and studying the Word of God. In that same letter, he also tells Timothy to "study to show thyself approved unto God, a workman that needeth not to be ashamed, rightly dividing the word of truth" (2 Timothy 2:15). Then he writes in 3:16-17, "All scripture is inspired by God and profitable for teaching, for reproof, for correction, for training in righteousness, so that the man of God may be adequately equipped for every good work." (2 Timothy 3:16-17, NASB) The Scripture is specifically speaking about the man of God (the leader) being taught, corrected, and trained in righteousness.

If we are to follow Paul's example, we should make it a priority to read the Bible. Leaders have to spend time with God reading His word. A helpful tool to use believers accountable for spending time reading God's Word is a Bible reading plan. There are many Bible reading plans on the internet. One that I find helpful is the 5x5x5 New Testament Reading Plan by Navigators ®.

While we must read the Bible, we can't stop there. We have to read other books also. The Bible doesn't tell us the books Paul was talking about, but we do know he read other books in addition to the Bible. After we have taken time to read God's word, let's expand our reading portfolio. What are some of the areas we should read? Leaders should read books on leadership, organizational development, church health, financing/budgeting, theology, communication, and teamwork, at the very least.

Book suggestion:

- *Christian Beliefs: Twenty Basics Every Christian Should Know* by Wayne Grudem

DISCIPLINE 2:

Being Secure In Your Leadership

☙

Do you wish to rise? Begin by descending. You plan a tower that will pierce the clouds? Lay first the foundation of humility.

- Augustine

The further I dug into Paul's life and ministry, the more I became certain that he was secure in his role as a leader for Jesus. Many leaders in the church are not secure in their roles. They feel inadequate, and they look for approval from people to validate their call to leadership, which is a big mistake.

This doesn't mean you will not have moments of doubt and uncertainty, because those things come with the territory of leadership. We can have those moments and still know that God has chosen us for the role we are in.

In the letter to the church in Galatia, Paul told of his call to apostleship. He writes,

"But when he who had set me apart before I was born, and who called me by his grace, was pleased to reveal his Son to me, in order that I might preach him among the Gentiles, I did not immediately consult with anyone; nor did I go up to Jerusalem to those who were apostles before me, but I went away into Arabia, and returned again to Damascus. Then after three years, I went up to Jerusalem to visit Cephas and remained with him fifteen days. But I saw none of the other apostles except James the Lord's brother." (Galatians 1:15-19, ESV)

Paul knew God had chosen him to lead, and it was God who called him by His grace. God wanted Paul to preach Jesus to the Gentiles. When Paul found out God was calling him to gospel preaching ministry, the first thing he did was to set out to do just that. He did not go and get approval from the apostolic leadership in Jerusalem on his call.

He went to the city of Damascus and began preaching Jesus to people who didn't have a relationship with him. If God has called you into a leadership role, your desire for approval and acceptance must ultimately come from him, not people. Leaders need to be secure in the fact that God has called and chosen them to lead.

Now allow me to add some balance to this. While we don't need people's approval to make us secure in our leadership, our leadership is developed while we are in community with other Christians, especially Christian leaders. Our call to lead will not develop properly without the training of current leaders. Christian leadership is not the place for a maverick or a lone ranger. Church leadership is a team sport.

Even though Paul didn't go to Jerusalem to get approval from the apostles who came before him, he did go to Damascus and join himself to a group of believers there. The book of Acts tells us, "Then was Saul (Paul) certain day with the disciples which were at Damascus" (Acts 9:19). It was in Damascus with other followers of Jesus that "he preached Christ in the synagogues" (Acts 9:22). It was while Paul was with the local church in that city that he "increased the more in strength and confounded the Jews which dwelt at Damascus." (Acts 9:22)

Even though your leadership isn't grounded in human approval, they do need to verify that your call to leadership is authentic and valid. When Paul finally did leave Damascus to go to Jerusalem, the church there didn't believe he had changed, and that he was a leader in the church.

It wasn't until Barnabas came and verified that Paul was a real Christian that the church in Jerusalem accepted him. Barnabas told them how Paul preached about Jesus boldly in Damascus (Acts 9:26-27). While people are not needed to validate our call to leadership, we need the church to help us develop our abilities to fulfill the call and verify that the call is real.

I remember when I accepted my call into the preaching ministry back in 1995. God had been dealing with me about preaching the gospel, so I went and set up a meeting with my pastor and told him what was going on. At that moment, he informed me that the Lord had already been dealing with him about me preaching the gospel. While talking to him, he verified that my call to ministry was real and began to train me to be a minister of the gospel of Jesus Christ.

DISCIPLINE 3:
Suffering Well For Jesus

☙

Good people must never expect to escape troubles; if they do, they will be disappointed, for none of their predecessors have been without them.

- C.H. Spurgeon

Suffering is a very difficult subject to talk about, especially in America. Many Christians in America are attempting to escape suffering. They are looking to Jesus to remove all pain and hardship. These requests are not in line with Scripture.

When Christians pray like this, we are praying outside of God's will. Especially when he has allowed the pain and suffering to come in the first place (Acts 8:1 – 3; Acts 14:22). That doesn't mean we shouldn't pray for relief and for hard times to end, because we can and should. But we must understand that God is not going to stop all pains, trials, and tribulations before they hit our lives.

Many American Christians have subscribed to the idea that God doesn't want them to endure any pain or to suffer any loss. Some of the blame for this worldview is that this message is taught on many popular radio stations and television networks, and by prominent pastors. It is the message that God wants everybody to be wealthy, healthy, and pain-free.

Please understand, I am not against being blessed or prospering in the name of the Lord. I believe that God wants to bless us and will take care of us, but that doesn't mean that Christians will not suffer. Suffering is a part of the agreement to follow Jesus and to make Him our Lord. Jesus even told us,

"I assure you that everyone who has given up house or brothers or sisters or mother or father or children or property, for my sake and for the Good News, will receive now in return a hundred times as many houses, brothers, sisters, mothers, children, and property—along with persecution. And in the world to come, that person will have eternal life." (Mark 10:29-30, NLT)

As the Scripture asserts, God wants to bless us, but the blessing comes with persecution and suffering. We, the leaders of the church, must tell Christians the whole truth; if you are going to follow Jesus, you will have to suffer for His name and fame. He requires it of His followers. We must tell people that suffering for Jesus is a part of the Christian life, but we as leaders must also suffer well to give them an example to follow.

This is what the Apostle Paul did. He suffered well for the name and fame of Jesus our Lord. Read what he writes to the church in Corinth in his second letter to them.

"We are pressed on every side by troubles, but we are not crushed. We are perplexed, but not driven to despair. We are hunted down, but never abandoned by God. We get knocked down, but we are not destroyed. Through suffering, our bodies continue to share in the death of Jesus so that the life of Jesus may also be seen in our bodies. Yes, we live under constant danger of death because we serve Jesus, so that the life of Jesus will be evident in our dying bodies. So we live in the face of death, but this has resulted in eternal life for you." (2 Corinthians 4:8-12, NLT)

The Apostle told them and us that it was through suffering Jesus was seen through their lives. He said the reason they were suffering was that he and his team were followers of Jesus. His motivation for enduring the suffering was two-fold; to show Jesus to others so people could receive eternal life - salvation. Paul endured the suffering because he wanted people to get saved. He wanted them to know the God he served. Leaders, we must do the same; we must suffer well so that Jesus can be seen in our lives and people can receive salvation that only Jesus provides.

In the passages above, Paul gives us a brief overview of what he endured to suffer for Jesus. But in the latter part of 2 Corinthians in chapter 11, he gets very specific about what he had to endure for the name and fame of Jesus so people could receive salvation. He wrote,

> Are they servants of Christ? I know I sound like a madman, but I have served him far more! I have worked harder, been put in prison more often, been whipped times without number, and faced death again and again. Five different times the Jewish leaders gave me thirty-nine lashes. Three times I was beaten with rods. Once I was stoned. Three times I was shipwrecked. Once I spent a whole night and a day adrift at sea. I have traveled on many long journeys. I have faced danger from rivers and from robbers.
>
> I have faced danger from my own people, the Jews, as well as from the Gentiles. I have faced danger in the cities, in the deserts, and on the seas.

And I have faced danger from men who claim to be believers but are not. I have worked hard and long, enduring many sleepless nights. I have been hungry and thirsty and have often gone without food. I have shivered in the cold, without enough clothing to keep me warm. Then, besides all this, I have the daily burden of my concern for all the churches. (2 Corinthians 11:23-28, NLT)

Wow! That's a lot. Let's list these out so we can be clear on what he endured:

1. Imprisoned often
2. Whipped too many times to count
3. Repeatedly faced death
4. Beaten five times with 39 lashes
5. Beaten with rods three times
6. Stoned once
7. Shipwrecked three times
8. Adrift at sea once
9. Traveled many long journeys
10. Faced danger in different places (river, cities, deserts, and seas)
11. Faced danger from people (robbers, the Jews, Gentiles, and false believers)

12. Many sleepless nights because of working hard with long hours
13. Often gone without food
14. Didn't have enough clothes to stay warm at times
15. Had the daily burden of concern for the all the churches.

My God, help us when we complain because something didn't go right, or the worship service didn't go exactly as planned, or someone was rude to us, and they took the parking spot we were eyeing. Father, help us when we grumble, get irritated, and become mean because someone doesn't like us or talk negatively about us. In the big scheme of things, we should thank God for allowing us to suffer in such a minor way for the name and fame of Jesus.

Even though Paul endured a lot of suffering, he didn't see it as punishment or as something out of the ordinary. As a matter of fact, when Paul thought about his suffering for Jesus, he called it "light momentary affliction." He also says in 2 Corinthians:

"For this light momentary affliction is preparing for us an eternal weight of glory beyond all comparison, as we look not to the things that are seen but to the things that are unseen. For the things that are seen are transient, but the things that are unseen are eternal." (2 Corinthians 4:17-18, ESV)

As he endured suffering, he had to keep the right perspective. He didn't focus on his situation or on the things he was going through. He focused his attention on what he would receive in the future - "an eternal weight of glory," which will be his reward for suffering for Jesus.

Leaders have to encourage the church to stop focusing so much on the things that are seen and are transient - things such as houses, cars, and money, because all of these things will pass away. We have to tell people to keep their focus on what they will receive in the future for suffering well for Jesus. They will receive a reward, "an eternal weight of glory," which will last for eternity.

What is the "eternal weight of glory" the Apostle kept his eyes on? I believe it was to reign with Jesus. Do you remember what Paul wrote to Timothy in his second letter about suffering? He wrote, "If we suffer, we shall also reign with him" (2 Timothy 2:12). To reign means to rule. Paul was looking toward ruling with Jesus, and suffering was just the process he had to go through to reap that reward.

You may be thinking, "What will he be reigning over with Jesus?" The story of the pounds in the gospel of Luke tells us the reward the servant received for doing the nobleman's request of increasing the pounds. The reward was to have authority (rule) over cities (Luke 19:12-27). He will rule over cities for Jesus. The Apostle John wrote Christians have been made "kings and priests unto God" (Revelation 1:6). What do kings do? They rule and have authority over land or territory. These lands are cities.

Leaders, we must remember that our suffering for Jesus is going to produce an eternal reward of ruling with him. We also must encourage our churches to suffer well so they, too, can have their portion to rule over with Jesus.

Book suggestion:

- *Jesus and The Disinherited* by Howard Thurman

DISCIPLINE 4:
Communication Is Essential

☙

> *A corrupt and unholy heart eventually will be exposed by corrupt and unholy speech… If the tongue is not controlled by God, it is a sure indicator that the heart is not, either.*
>
> **- John MacArthur**

When I was planting Triumphant Assembly and trying to figure out how to become a better leader, the books that I read on leadership made a point to emphasize the leader's need to be good at communication. In particular, being good at communicating vision. They point out the importance of consistently communicating the vision God gave you for the local church and the necessity for the leader to believe in the vision as well to speak with conviction. The reason is, if the leader doesn't believe in the vision, it will be difficult for the congregation to believe in it.

I would affirm the need to clearly communicate the vision to others. Yet, I believe if we leave the conversation there, when it comes to church leadership, we will be doing the leaders in the local church a huge disservice. As I continued to investigate the leadership principles in the ministry of the Apostle Paul, I came across three other areas of communication he focused on when he wrote to churches. Those three areas are: sharing the gospel of Jesus, courageous confrontation, and organizational communication.

While I believe everyone who is a follower of Jesus should be able to tell someone how they can give their life to Jesus, it is a must that leaders in the local church be able to share the gospel with people. They should be able to tell people who Jesus is (The God/Man); what he has done (His sinless life, death, and resurrection for humanity's sin against God) and how others can receive the benefit of what Jesus has done (Repent of sin, belief in this message, and confess Jesus as Lord).

Not only should we be able to tell the gospel, we also should be eager to share the story of Jesus. We should want to tell people about Jesus and be ready to do so when the opportunity presents itself. Leaders have to be able to tell people the gospel.

1. Informing people of John 3:16, how "God so loved the world that he gave his only begotten son that whosoever believeth in him should not perish but have everlasting life."

2. Letting them know Jesus declared in Luke 13:3 that if they don't repent of their sin and turn to God, they will perish for eternity.

3. Sharing Romans 10:9 with them, that if they confess Jesus as their Lord and believe that God has raised Him from the dead, they will be saved.

Also helping them to understand Ephesians 2:8-9 "for by grace are you saved through faith; and that not of yourselves: it is the gift of God: not of works, lest any man should boast." Salvation is a precious gift from God, that can't be worked for to receive, or maintained. They are saved by grace alone, through faith alone, through Jesus's finished work only.

Remember, one of Jesus's primary goals for His disciples is to become "fishers of men" (Matthew. 4:19). He wants His followers to influence people through our words and deeds so we can share the gospel with them. The words of the gospel shouldn't just be communicated out of our mouths and not lived out in our lives. When people see a disparity between our words and deeds, it becomes difficult to influence them because they see a lack of integrity.

While our integrity is crucial, we will not be perfect, sinless while we are in these mortal bodies. As well, no one has ever been saved by looking at someone's lifestyle. Our lives can validate our belief in Jesus in the eyes of people, but our lives can not save people. Therefore, we must remember we have to tell people the gospel of Jesus Christ. The Scripture declares, "faith cometh by hearing and hearing by the word of God" (Romans 10:17).

A helpful process to use when sharing the gospel with people is the Romans' Road. The Romans' Road process uses verses from the book of Romans to help them see their need for Jesus and how they can receive salvation. The scriptures that are used are:

- 3:23
- 5:8
- 6:23
- 10:9-10
- 10:13

Not only must we tell this good news to people who don't know Jesus, but we must also tell it to people who already know him. The Apostle Paul writes, "So as much as in me is, I am ready to preach the gospel to you that are at Rome also. For I am not ashamed of the gospel of Christ: for it is the power of God unto salvation to every one that believeth." (Romans 1:15-16)

The Apostle writes he was "ready to preach the gospel." He was eager to preach in Rome about Jesus and what he has done for humanity. What I find interesting is that this verse is written to Christians, not non-believers. He was telling people who already believed the gospel of Jesus Christ that he was eager to preach this message of good news to them as well. We know he eagerly looked for opportunities to tell non-believers about Jesus, but he also had a desire to tell the church.

The church needs to hear the gospel, just like those who have not believed in Jesus. The only difference is the purpose of preaching the message. The church needs to hear the message to build its faith. The non-believers need to hear the message so they can receive the faith. The church must hear the gospel to remind them of how great, awesome, and merciful God is. The non-believers must hear the gospel so they can recognize how great, awesome, and merciful God is.

That's why at Triumphant Assembly, we shared the gospel of Jesus at every worship service. We used our worship services as one entry point for people to experience our ministry and hear the gospel. Therefore, no matter who was in our worship service, believer or non-believer, they will hear the gospel being preached.

The Apostle Paul was ready to share the gospel with Christians and non-Christians alike. He was even ready to let Christians know when they were not living according to the gospel. To do this, not only must you be courageous, but you must also be compassionate. You must care for other followers of Jesus.

For a leader to be courageous, two areas must be addressed. First, they must move past their desire to be affirmed by people, which will also require them to move past the fear of being seen as a dictator, being rejected, and losing members.

The other area if their love for people. Leaders in the church must love people and want to see them grow in their relationship with Christ. The type of love is a sacrificial love. The kind of love where we sacrifice our feelings and image to tell people the truth in love.

The concept of telling the truth in love is a simple concept, but it can be difficult to practice. As leaders, we must tell the truth (say what the Bible says) about sin and people's actions, including our own. But that honesty must be covered in love and respect for the dignity of others.

We are not attacking the person but speaking on their action. We are not condemning the Christian while letting them know their actions are wrong. The goal is not to leave them beat up and discouraged. Our communication goals should be to build them up and equip them to live better for Jesus. Our words must be kind and firm. Encouraging, yet straightforward. Honest, but not rude and sarcastic.

This is what the Apostle Paul did to the Apostle Peter at the church in Antioch. He was lovingly courageous when he confronted Peter in front of the whole church. Peter had come to Antioch to fellowship with the church. While he was there, he wasn't practicing the dietary ordinances of the Jews, and he was mingling with the Gentile believers.

While Peter was there, the Apostle James sent delegates from Jerusalem to Antioch to see how the church was doing. While they were there, the Apostle Peter returned to dietary practices of Jews, and withdrew himself from the Gentile believers. Peter's influence was so strong that one of the main leaders in the church in Antioch, Barnabas, followed in him.

The Apostle Peter's actions were causing division in the local church.

Read what the Apostle Paul wrote about this moment.

"But when Cephas came to Antioch, I opposed him to his face, because he stood condemned… But when I saw that they were not straightforward about the truth of the gospel, I said to Cephas in the presence of all, 'If you being a Jew, live like the Gentiles and not like the Jews, how is it that you compel the Gentiles to live like Jews?'" (Galatians 2:11, 14; NASB)

Let's examine what Paul did. He didn't go to the believers from Jerusalem. Nor did he go to Barnabas. Paul went to the individual who was starting the division within the church. He spoke to Peter face to face about his behavior. He addressed Peter openly in front of the church for everyone to hear.

As we leaders, there will be times when leaders will have to openly confront and correct people. Then other times, those face-to-face conversations will be in private, or with two or three mature believers present. As we can see, Paul was not attacking Peter as a person, but addressing his inconsistent behavior.

In order to have these types of conversations, the leader has to be courageous and loving. I believe it took a lot of courage to confront the Apostle Peter, a major figure in the church, in front of the whole congregation at Antioch. Yet it also took a lot of love, because Paul didn't want the followers of Jesus to receive the wrong message and be misled. Paul loved them more than he loved his own comfort and security.

After a leader understands the importance of sharing the gospel and courageous confrontation in love, then things like the importance of communicating organizational structure (such as vision, mission, and systems) can be addressed. The Apostle Paul also talked about how things should operate in the local church. Look at his letter to the church in Ephesus. The epistle to the Ephesians is broken up into two major portions.

Chapters 1 – 3 are the theological aspects of the church. I call it the "big picture stuff". He writes about the grace of God, the meaning of being a Christian, spiritual gifts, and so on. This is the portion of the book where he tells them, and us, who we are and what we are to strive for. The Apostle Paul (the leader) is basically telling the church its mission and vision.

Then in chapters 4 – 6, he tells them how to live out their faith in Jesus in a practical way. He writes on how Christian unity operates, how families are to live with each other, how to wage spiritual warfare, and more. This is a systems conversation. Basically, this is how the church of Jesus Christ is supposed to operate.

Leaders must be able to communicate the big-picture stuff as well as the systems of the organization. The systems are the practical processes we will use within the fellowship to complete the mission and vision of the local church.

All leaders are supposed to bring order to chaos. Every letter in the New Testament was addressed to a church that had a problem. Problems are not new to the church. Problems come automatically when people come together to do life together. It's normal. When leaders talk about mission, vision, and systems, they are bringing order to chaos, or, at the very least, to something that could become chaotic.

When the Apostle Paul wrote to Titus while Titus is in Crete, he told him to bring order (organization) to the church there. He writes,

"For this cause left I thee in Crete, that thou shouldest set in order the things that are wanting, and ordain elders in every city, as I had appointed thee." (Titus 1:5)

Paul wanted him to "set in order the things that are wanting." The things that are wanting are things that are lacking. Those things or areas were incorrect and out of order. There was a part of the church in Crete that wasn't organized, and Paul wanted Titus to bring some order to it. Paul wanted him to fix those problems.

From an organizational standpoint, the only way to fix those problems is to put a structure in place with processes. Paul also lets him know that while the Cretan church needs structure with processes (systems), they also need people to keep the structure and systems in place when he leaves. Therefore, he needs to "ordain elders in every city." These elders were the local church leaders who followed the structure and systems he put in place.

When we look at Scripture, the elder is a specific title (position) in the church. It's a position with qualifications and responsibilities. We also see more positions with qualifications listed in the Bible, such as Apostles, Prophets, Evangelists, and Pastors and Teachers, which is in Ephesians 4:11 – 16. Then in 1Timothy 3:1-13 Paul writes about the bishop and the deacon along with their qualifications and requirements.

My point in bringing this up is not to debate which offices are still operational today, but the very fact that the Apostle Paul talked about positions with duties. When we talk about organizational structure, we can't leave out titles and their responsibilities. The church leader, especially the church planting leader, must establish a structure within the local church by incorporating positions.

These positions must have specific qualifications and requirements as this will help bring order to chaos. People need to know who is responsible for what area and for what system. They need to know who they are going to report to for ministry responsibilities and what they are being held accountable to.

Book suggestion:

- *Connect Grow Serve Go* by Bret Robbe and Dwayne McCrary

DISCIPLINE 5:
Entrepreurial Visionary

☙

God loves with a great love the man whose heart is bursting with a passion for the impossible.

- William Booth

I am of the firm conviction that leaders are risk-takers. They are not willing or interested in going with the flow in order not to rock the boat. There are times when the boat has to be rocked, and the one that has the most leverage to do it is the leader. The rocking may be to add innovation to how the church operates.

Church leaders must be willing to innovate. We must be willing to try new systems and programs to reach more people for Jesus. This will also require leaders to stop some activities or allow them to die because they aren't working.

When I think about the Apostle Paul, I think of a risk-taker, an entrepreneur. He was not satisfied with the status quo, ministry-as-usual mentality. Paul was interested in going places where others had not been and were not interested in going. He went to, and wanted to go to, uncharted territories for Jesus. He wrote in the book of Romans,

"And thus I aspired to preach the gospel, not where Christ was already named, so that I would not build on another man's foundation." (Roman 15:20)

On the surface that can sound egotistical, but that is not it at all. Paul's mentality, I believe, was that if Jesus has been preached there already, more than likely, a church has already been started in that area. He wanted to find a place where no one had heard of Jesus, so people and get saved and start a church there. The Apostle made it clear that this was his aspiration. This was his desire and motivation. He has a desire to fill a void in the earth.

There were, and still are, people who haven't heard of Jesus and His finished work on the cross for humanity, so he wanted to go there and tell them about it. He wanted to reach those who haven't been reached. That's entrepreneurship at its very core.

When I looked at my task as a church planter in Cleveland, OH, I had to be entrepreneurial. My aspiration was to fill a void in the earth with the gospel of Jesus Christ. I wanted to reach people who were far from God and didn't have a relationship with him through His Son, Jesus. To do that, along with my local fellowship, we had to take risks and do ministry a little differently.

For example, instead of wearing a formal suit for worship services, I dressed more relaxed so people who didn't have suits would feel more comfortable in our worship service. While this may be a small change for some, in the African American church culture around 2009-10 in Cleveland, OH wearing suits was the norm, and generally, the more expensive the suit, the better.

We weren't satisfied with the status quo of ministry as usual. But we are not being different for the sake of being different. We were being different and taking risks to reach people who didn't know Jesus. Everything we did was an attempt to help someone become a disciple of Jesus. This is how the Apostle Paul puts it:

> To the Jew I became as a Jew, so that I might win Jews; to those who are under the Law, as under the Law though not being myself under the Law, so that I might win those who are under the Law, to those who are without laws, as without law, though not being without the law of God but under the

law of Christ, so that I might win those who are without law. To the weak became I as weak, that I might gain the weak: I am made all things to all men, that I might, by all means, save some. (1 Corinthians 9:20 – 22; NASB)

The Apostle Paul took risks and was flexible as a church planter to attempt to reach multiple groups of people. That was unique about his ministry. Even though he was the Apostle to the Gentiles, he didn't just focus on the Gentiles. Whenever he went into a different city, he first talked to the Jews; then he went to the Gentiles.

He took the risk to diversify his target audience so that he could reach as many people as he could. He knew he wasn't going to help everyone he met get saved, but he could help some. As a church planter, I knew everyone was not going to get saved through Triumphant Assembly, and everyone was not going to become a member of our local fellowship, but we still needed to take some risk to help some folks come to know Jesus.

The Apostle Paul also wanted to reach as many people as he could by going as far as he could. In the book of Romans, he told his readers his aspiration of reaching people for Jesus in Spain. "Therefore, when

I finished this, and have put my seal on this fruit of theirs, I will go on by way of you to Spain." (Romans 15:28)

That is the very essence of vision. Paul's vision to go to Spain was driven by his mission to reach as many people as he could for Jesus. He wanted to go to the other side of the known world at that time, The Roman Empire, and plant local church fellowships. While some speculate, he reached Spain; most scholars believe he didn't. He died in Rome without reaching his vision. Yet, he died with vision in his heart and mission on his mind.

Every senior church leader must have a vision for the local church they lead. They should know where or what they want the church to be in the future (in accordance with Scripture). The vision must be a compelling image of the future that grips the leader's heart.

The leader has to answer the question, "Where are we trying to go?" When I saw Triumphant Assembly in the future, I saw a multi-ethnic fellowship of believers worshipping God together, looking like heaven.

"After this I saw a vast crowd, too great to count, from every nation and tribe and people and language, standing in front of the throne and before the Lamb.

They were clothed in white robes and held palm branches in their hands. And they were shouting with a great roar, "Salvation comes from our God who sits on the throne and from the Lamb!" (Revelation 7:9 – 10, NLT)

Then our mission fueled our vision. The question the leader has to answer for the mission is, "Why do we want to do this?" At Triumphant Assembly, our mission was "to make disciples of Jesus who love God and love people." Our mission comes from the Great Commandment and the Great Commission.

The Great Commandment is found in Matthew 22:37 – 40:

"Jesus replied, "You must love the Lord your God with all your heart, all your soul, and all your mind. This is the first and greatest commandment. A second is equally important: Love your neighbor as yourself. All the other commandments and all the demands of the prophets are based on these two commandments." (NLT)

The Great Commission is in Matthew 28:18 – 20:

"Jesus came and told his disciples, "I have been given complete authority in heaven and on earth. Therefore, go and make disciples of all the nations, baptizing them in the name of the Father and the Son and the Holy Spirit. Teach these new disciples to obey all the commands I have given you. And be sure of this: I am with you always, even to the end of the age." (NLT)

When we looked at these Scriptures, we saw what it meant to make disciples of Jesus. We taught the church that disciples of Jesus must love God, connect to the church, serve in the kingdom, reach out to the world, and lead others. We believed the disciples that would eventually fill up our church would be from different ethnic backgrounds, different ages, different cultures, different economic statues, and different skin colors.

Even though Triumphant Assembly isn't in existence anymore, it is still my focus as a church leader, and it is the vision and mission at Mt. Calvary Baptist Church where I currently pastor. If you want to find out more about our vision, mission, and discipleship process, get a copy of my book, *The Next Leader*.

Book suggestion:

- *The Next Leader* by Stephen Owens

DISCIPLINE 6:
Focus On Leadership Duplication

☙

> *Leadership training cannot be done on a mass scale. It requires patient, careful instruction and prayerful, personal guidance over a considerable time. Disciples are not manufactured wholesale. They are produced only one by one, because someone has taken the pains to disciple, to instruct and enlighten, to nurture and train one that is younger.*
>
> **- Oswald Sanders**

A primary component the local church must focus on is leadership duplication. I believe the local church is the best place to learn how to become a leader in the church. Aspiring church leaders must be able to receive biblical teaching and leadership training and then have the opportunity to apply what they have learned. The optimum place to do this is in the context of the local church fellowship under the supervision of senior leadership.

I am not discounting the work of colleges, seminaries, and para-church organizations because they are also able to help develop leaders. However, they should be seen as secondary avenues for church leadership development, not primary sources. We must focus on developing future church leaders from within our congregations.

The concept of leadership is near and dear to my heart. I have a passion for developing and duplicating leaders for the kingdom of God. My heart is to help leaders magnify Jesus in word and deed. The primary way I am focusing on developing and duplicating leaders is through our local church. This is being done through an apprenticeship model.

At Triumphant Assembly, we began talking about leadership opportunities to people as soon as they commit their lives to Jesus and join our fellowship. In our new members' class (The T.A. DNA), we informed them that we believed every believer in Christ had the potential to become a leader in Triumphant Assembly. This didn't mean that every believer was going to elder, a deacon, or on the executive staff. But it did mean that they may lead a ministry, small group, a service project, or an outreach project.

To become a leader, they had to go through our systems (Growth Track, Discipleship Process, and the Apprenticeship Process). The Growth Track was our new member assimilation process. The Discipleship Process is the steps every member should take as they mature as a disciple of Jesus.

The apprenticeship process is where an aspiring leader helps a current leader grow a ministry team or small group. The apprentice leader's responsibilities were to learn from the leader, assist the leader in doing effective ministry, and execute leadership tasks when received. This process was at least 6 months. Remember what I wrote at the beginning of this book? *If you can't follow well, you will not be able to lead well.*

We were using the local church as a training ground for the next generation of leaders. This wasn't a quick process; it would take years to raise up multiple leaders. Nevertheless, I believe it will be worth it in the long run. I still believe it. We use the same process at Mt. Calvary Baptist Church, which is also discussed in *The Next Leader*.

It was and is my prayer that many of those leaders would be sent to plant churches, become pastors of established churches, and help other churches grow. For the leaders who would stay with us, I was praying they would help us become effective and reach more people, and help them grow in their faith. As well as many of them becoming leaders in the marketplace by becoming entrepreneurs, starting non-profits, climbing the corporate ladder, and so forth. I am convinced that followers of Jesus should be leaders in the church as well as in the marketplace.

The Apostle Paul understood the concept of leadership duplication. As I reviewed the Apostle's life and writings, a major component of developing future leaders was done through apprenticeship. Apprenticeship occurs when someone wants to learn a craft (the apprentice) from someone who has mastered the craft (master craftsman).

The apprentice learns by observation and practice under the supervision of a skilled laborer. While no one has completely mastered the craft of leadership, current leaders in the local church can train, develop, guide, encourage, correct, and assist new leaders in the art of church leadership.

When we look at Scripture, we can see the Apostle Paul saw himself as a master craftsman. This is what he wrote about himself in the first epistle to the church in Corinth. He writes, "According to the grace of God given to me, like a skilled master builder I laid a foundation, and someone else is building upon it.

Let each one take care how he builds upon it." (1 Corinthians 3:10; ESV)

He saw himself as a "wise master builder." He was competent in the craft of building (he knows what to do and how to do it), had tons of experience in building, and could help others learn to build. A helpful thing to remember is just because a person is a master builder, that does not mean he or she can do whatever they want during the building process.

In actuality, the very opposite is done. The master-builder knows the importance of a plan and using it during construction. They rely on the blueprint for direction. We as leaders must do the same thing; making sure we are relying on the blueprint of Scripture as we are assisting God in building future leaders. As well as learning from of church leaders who have processes in place to develop spiritually healthy leaders.

The question that has to be asked is, how did Paul become a "wise master builder?" The only way he could have done it was to be an apprentice to a current builder. Who was that builder? His name was Joseph. He was given the nickname of Barnabas by the apostles in Jerusalem.

In Acts chapter 11, Barnabas is sent to the church in Antioch by the church in Jerusalem. When he arrived, the Scripture says he "saw the grace of God" on the church, and he encouraged them (Acts 11:23). Then in verse 25 of the same chapter, Barnabas leaves Antioch in search for a new believer named Saul (Apostle Paul) in Tarsus. When Barnabas found Saul, he brought him back to Antioch, and they taught there for a year.

During their time there, Barnabas was the more experienced leader, not Saul. They were Barnabas and Saul, not Saul and Barnabas. As a matter of fact, when the Holy Spirit sent them out on their first missionary journey, the Spirit said, "Separate me Barnabas and Saul" (Acts 13:2), indicating that Saul was not the master craftsman, but the apprentice. Paul developed his church building skills under an experienced builder - Barnabas.

Then, when it was Paul's turn to lead as a master craftsman, he followed the same apprentice model. He allowed a future leader to become his apprentice, and that was Timothy (his son in the ministry). On Paul's second missionary journey while he was with Silas, they came to a city called Lystra, and they were informed of a young man named Timothy. His mother was Jewish, and his father was Greek.

Timothy had a good reputation among the brethren in Lystra and Iconium. When Paul heard about Timothy and his character, he allowed him to tag along with his team (Acts 16:1 – 3). Timothy finished the second journey with Paul and his team. Then he went with Paul on his third journey. Timothy was received on-the-job training.

Timothy was even given the great opportunity to write multiple books with the Apostle Paul.

1. "Paul an apostle of Jesus Christ ... and Timothy our brother" – 2 Corinthians 1:1
2. "Paul an apostle of Jesus Christ... and Timothy our brother" – Colossians 1:1
3. "Paul, and Silvanus, and Timothy" – 1 Thessalonians 1:1
4. "Paul, and Silvanus, and Timothy" – 2 Thessalonians 1:1
5. "Paul, a prisoner of Jesus Christ, and Timothy our brother" – Philemon 1

Then the Apostle Paul sent out Timothy to do ministry at multiple churches. In Acts 19:22 Paul sent him to Macedonia. Paul also sent his to Ephesus to serve the church. (1 Timothy 1:3). Eventually, Timothy became the bishop over the church in Ephesus. The whole time Timothy was with Paul and his team, he was being trained for leadership.

In the second letter Paul writes to Timothy, he told Timothy to make sure he focused some of his time on leadership development and duplication as well. Paul wanted him to concentrate on building leaders who will be able to build future leaders. Paul wrote,

"The things which you have heard from me in the presence of many witnesses, entrust these to faithful men who will be able to teach others also." (2 Timothy 2:2; NASB)

This is leadership duplication at its very best. In this Scripture, there are four generations of leaders shown. There is the Apostle Paul, which is the 1st generation who told the message to Timothy. Then there is Timothy, which is the 2nd generation who heard the message and told it to faithful men.

These faithful men are the 3rd generation of leaders who were commissioned to teach the message to others. The others are the 4th generation, and they are unknown leaders who would come in the future. Now that's creating a leadership pipeline. If we focus our effects on developing those who will, in turn, focus on developing others, lives will be changed, and we will always have faithful leaders in the local church.

Book suggestion:

- *The New One Minute Manager* by Ken Blanchard and Spencer Johnson

DISCIPLINE 7:
Team-Base Ministry

☙

Satan always hates Christian fellowship; it is his policy to keep Christians apart. Anything which can divide saints from one another he delights in. He attaches far more importance to godly intercourse than we do. Since union is strength, he does his best to promote separation.

- C.H. Spurgeon

As mentioned before, ministry is a team sport. Leaders must view themselves as part of a team. Too many leaders see themselves as lone rangers or soloists. When a leader thinks like that, they have a big ego and eventually they burn out. As a ministry grows it becomes too much for one person to handle.

Many times, when I listen to pastors and church planters talk about leadership, the one animal they consistently point to is the eagle. Reason being that the eagle is seen as a visionary bird. They can see far into the distance as well as having a clear vision to see prey that are on the ground. They also have the great ability to soar high in the sky. I understand these pastors want to make sure leaders are visionaries, and they will rise above the mundane issues to see where the organization must go.

Yet, if we leave the conversation there, we will leave future leaders with incomplete information. Eagles have a keen vision and can fly high, but they are also very isolated animals. They are generally seen by themselves. They fly by themselves, and they hunt by themselves.

As I observe leaders, pastors, and church planters, in particular, they resemble the eagles not only in their respectable qualities, but also in their inferior qualities. Many leaders are isolated and lonely. They don't value building relationships with other leaders. Therefore, they feel the pressure and burden of leadership all alone when they could have allowed others in the organization to share the burden with them.

That's why I will not only talk about the attributes of the eagle, but I will also tell aspiring leaders about the lion, the king of the jungle. I like to discuss lions because while they may be vulnerable creatures by themselves when they are in a group (the pride), they can take down any animal in the jungle. Even though there may be a leader within the pride, they still fight as a group, as a team. They conquer territory and maintain it because they work as a team. I believe leaders must raise up other lions that will be able to fight alongside them. In that way, the team, the group, can carry the burden of the ministry together.

Here is the reality in building a team; it is hard work. It takes time, patience, trust, and confrontation. You don't just deal with your issues; you have to deal with the issues of your teammates. When things affect someone's life, it can impact the team's effect.

I have made many mistakes in team building. I have chosen the wrong people for the wrong jobs. I made the big mistake of focusing on competency over character. I have not said things to people when I should have confronted them. Believe me, I have made my share of mistakes when it comes to team building, and I know I will make many more. But I am committed to doing ministry as a team and training my leaders to do ministry as a team.

When we look at Scripture, I believe this concept of team-based ministry is shown clearly. We can begin with the ministry of Jesus, the Lion of the tribe of Judah. Jesus did team-based ministry. While the responsibility of the church and its future rested on his shoulders, he did not do ministry by himself. He let his future leaders participate in some of the responsibilities.

In the Gospel of John, we see that a part of Jesus's ministry included water baptism. The Apostle John tells us that Jesus's ministry had baptized more people than John the Baptist. But what is interesting is that the Apostle John tells us that Jesus wasn't the one baptizing the people; it was the disciples (John 4:1– 2). Jesus allowed them to carry a portion of the burden with him.

Then we see in Matthew chapter 10, Jesus sent out the twelve as a team to do ministry. Jesus, the Lion of Judah, sent them out as a group to minister to the lost sheep of Israel. (Matthew 10:5) In this instance, we see Jesus using team-based ministry with a significant amount of people, twelve individuals.

Yet, when we turn to Mark's account of the ministry of Jesus, Mark shows Jesus at another time sending out the twelve, not as one collective group, but in pairs of two. (Mark 6:7) Finally, we see Jesus using the team-based model again in Luke 10:1 when He sends out the 70 in pairs of two to do ministry in the cities where he was going to go.

Now let's turn our attention to the Book of Acts to see how the Apostle Paul valued team-based ministry. The Apostle was a part of a team-based ministry early on in his apostolic career. He first joined Barnabas' team in Acts 11:25 – 30 and helped build the church in Antioch.

As a team, Barnabas and Paul taught many people about Jesus. They also took money to the church in Jerusalem from Antioch when a great famine hit the city of Jerusalem. Then Acts chapter 13 tells us that "Paul and his team" had sailed from Paphos to go to Perga in Pamphylia (Acts 13:13).

In Acts 15, Barnabas and Paul decided to split up their team. This was not done so that they might minister as individuals, because they still used team-based ministry. They both chose new people to be a part of their different teams. The Scripture says Barnabas took John Mark and Paul chose Silas to be on his team (Acts 15:39 – 40). Then in chapter 16 we see Luke join the Apostle Paul's team. Luke ends up writing how a young lady with an evil spirit followed "Paul's team" around the city of Thyatira (Acts 16:17). This is another reference to the Apostle Paul using team-based ministry.

When Paul sent out Timothy to do ministry, he did not send Timothy out by himself. He sent Erastus along with him to Macedonia so they can serve the church as a team. (Acts 19:22) Team-based ministry is crucial if you want to be effective as a leader. There is no substitute for it. Leaders who have a solo mentality will burn out fast and will build unhealthy organizations.

DISCIPLINE 8:
Don't Be Afraid To Talk About Money

☙

> *There cannot be a surer rule, nor a stronger exhortation to the observance of it, than when we are taught that all the endowments which we possess are divine deposits entrusted to us for the very purpose of being distributed for the good of our neighbor.*
>
> **- John Calvin**

When I got to the topic of money when I prepared for my leadership class, I questioned if I should include it among the disciplines. The reason being, there are many leaders in the church that will not be involved with handling money in the local assembly. They will not have to talk about it, teach on it, count it, or be concerned if there is enough money to operate the church effectively. But I concluded while every leader may not have to deal with money within the local church, every leader in the church should know the importance of money within the local church context.

Though we don't look to money as a god, it is an important part of doing ministry well for the glory of God. Money is needed for a lot of things in the church, like buying Bibles, paying bills, and funding salaries, mission trips, and missionaries. The Scriptures have a lot to say concerning money.

Therefore, leaders in the church can't be afraid to talk about money or teach on it in church. When I first planted Triumphant Assembly as a small-group Bible study, I was very hesitant to ask for an offering. The only thing that kept going through my mind was, "what are these people going to think and say if I raise an offering?"

Thank God he sent someone into the Bible study who asked openly if we were going to take up an offering. When I saw that people wanted to give to the cause of Christ, my boldness grew as well as my teaching on the subject. I am so glad God works despite the frailties and hesitancies of the leaders he chooses.

Future leaders and congregations must know what God says about money in His word. When we look at the

Apostle Paul, he was not afraid to talk to the churches he planted about money and giving. Let's turn our attention to the two letters he wrote to the church in Corinth. In 1st Corinthians chapter 9, Paul told them about the importance of paying those who feed them spiritually by preaching God's word. Read what he writes:

"Just as farm workers who plow fields and thresh the grain expect a share of the harvest, Christian workers should be paid by those they serve." (1 Corinthians 9:10, NLT)

He goes on to let them know, because they (Barnabas and Paul), have sowed spiritual things, preaching the word of God, to the church that they should in return sow carnal things, money, to them. Paul was not saying this because he was looking for a handout. He was a bi-vocational church planter (Acts 18:3). He intentionally worked making tents to be an example to the Christians in the church plants.

He even tells the Corinthians in verse 12 of chapter 9, how they (Barnabas and Paul) had not used that right to be paid among them because they did not want to hinder the "gospel of Christ." But just because they didn't request what was rightfully due to them does not mean it wasn't due them. They chose not to exercise the privilege at that moment.

Like the Apostle Paul, the senior leaders should not be afraid to talk about compensation. Yet, they must temper their conversation with knowledge of the church's financial abilities. If the church is not currently bringing in enough to pay a salary for the pastor, then the pastor may have to go and make tents until the church is financially stable enough. But if the church as the ability to pay a pastoral salary, they should.

Another option is to seek to raise funds from outside of the church. Maybe from a church-planting agencies, sponsoring churches, and individuals who want to support the mission of the church, though they are not a member. Whether or not the pastor receives salary, the congregation must be taught that "the Lord ordained that they which preach the gospel should live of the gospel" (1 Corinthians 9:14). The NLT puts it a little clearer: "The Lord gave orders that those who preach the Good News should be supported by those who benefit from it."

Then in chapter 16, Paul told the church in Corinth about the importance of being a benevolent congregation, and they regularly collect an offering. In the first verse, he told them they should collect money for the needy Christians in Jerusalem. Collecting money for those in need and to helps other churches allow the congregation to take their minds off of their individual fellowship and concentrate more on the mission of God.

It will help them understand that the church of Jesus Christ is bigger than their local assembly, and God is doing amazing things among other Christ followers in other areas. Then in verse two, Paul lets them know that they should be collecting offerings every week among themselves. Leaders should tell the church that they should have money set aside to give to further the mission of God and to support the local work of the ministry.

Leaders must also tell the church about the blessing that comes from God when they give. The Apostle Paul tells the leaders (elders) at the church in Ephesus as he leaves them in Acts 20:35, "remember the words of the Lord Jesus, how he said, It is more blessed to give than to receive." (KJV) Therefore, it is the responsibility of the leaders of the church to tell the congregation about the blessing that comes with giving. Please realize that this isn't a get-rich-quick scheme. It's biblical teaching concerning Christian stewardship.

In the second letter Paul writes to the church in Corinth, he told them about the ministry of giving. In chapter nine, he wrote, "he which sows sparingly will also reap sparingly, and he which sows bountifully will also reap bountifully" (2 Corinthians 9:6, NKJV). He is letting them know that people who give money should give with an expectation of a harvest.

But the harvest is contingent primarily upon the quantity their giving, sparingly or bountifully. Depending on how much they give, they will either be blessed with a small harvest or a large one. But no matter how much they give, they will be blessed in return.

Then in verse seven of the same chapter, he lets them know their harvest is also dependent on the quality of their giving. He wrote, "let each one give as he purposes in his heart, not grudgingly or of necessity; for God loves a cheerful giver" (NKJV). He was teaching the church that Christians should have a desire to give.

They should give out of a merry heart, not because it's a requirement or because they feel pressured to give. Believers should give because we're able, not because we must. Besides, this is how God wants to see us give in the first place - cheerfully.

As I look at the Apostle Paul and how he wasn't ashamed to talk about money, I believe he was following in the footsteps of Jesus. Jesus had no issues with talking about money and worldly possessions. When we read his parables, we find out that a fourth of them dealt with how to use money, possessions and wealth. If we think about it, if Jesus was physically pastoring a local church right now, at least one Sunday a month he would deal with some aspect of money and worldly possessions.

The reason he would do this is that he knows the human heart has a tendency toward elevating possessions and wealth over of their proper place. As humans, we are prone to turning things into idols and live with them. The one area humanity constantly does this in is the area of finances. A good sermon series or group of bible study lessons to have is to spend time on the parables where Jesus talked about money and worldly possession.

Even Christians are susceptible to making money into an idol and worshipping it by doing anything to get more of it (Matthew 6:24). Leaders, we must follow in the path of Jesus and Paul. We cannot be afraid to teach on the potential dangers of idolatry in the areas of money, wealth, and possessions.

Book suggestion:
- *The Grace of Giving* by John Stott and Chris Wright

DISCIPLINE 9:
The Goal Is To Finish

‿

Courage is not simply one of the virtues, but the form of every virtue at the testing point.

- C.S. Lewis

The last discipline we are going to deal with focuses on persistence and faithfulness. I believe this has to be discussed because the number of pastoral leaders throwing their hands up and quitting the ministry is mind-blowing.

As of January 2022, it is estimated that 1.5% of US pastors leave the pastorate annually.[1] That is a staggering number when you consider its estimated that there are 380,000 protestant churches in America.[2] That's around 5,700 leaders not finishing. I don't know about, but that's a large number of pastors leaving the ministry every year. This is due to a combination of church conflicts, moral failure, burnout, and being forced to leave by the church. I am praying that God will help us to stay in the fight for righteousness, and to walk in holiness in the process.

It is important that we encourage leaders and future leaders to finish well. We must strive with the help of the Holy Spirit to complete the tasks God has given us, no matter how difficult it becomes. I believe it goes back to understanding how to suffer well for Jesus and not quitting too soon.

I am not saying that it's going to be easy, nor am I making light of the task at hand, but I have a great desire to hear God tell me, "Well done, good and faithful servant; you have been faithful over a few things, I will make you ruler over many things. Enter into the joy of your lord." (Matthew 25:23, NKJV)

When I look at the Apostle Paul, he wasn't a quitter. He didn't stop leading, preaching, teaching, and planting churches just because things became difficult. I believe he didn't quit because he was leading for something bigger than himself. He was leading for Jesus.

He wanted the name and fame of Jesus to be spread throughout the earth. He was also leading to receive his future reward of reigning with Christ. Personally, I don't believe we talk enough about the rewards Christians will receive for sacrificing our lives for Jesus. These are the words of the Apostle Paul to the leaders at Ephesus,

> Now, behold, bound in spirit, I am on my way to Jerusalem, not knowing what will happen to me there except that the Holy Spirit solemnly testifies to me in every city, saying, that bonds and afflictions await me. But I do not consider my life of any account as dear to myself so that I may finish my course and the ministry which I received from the Lord Jesus, to testify solemnly of the gospel of the grace of God. (Acts 20:22 – 24, NASB)

The King James Version has the beginning portion of verse 24 as "But none of these things moves me." We must understand what he is saying. He is telling them, and us, that no matter what happens, he is going to complete the ministry Jesus has given him. Bonds (jail and chains) are not going to stop him from finishing. Nor will afflictions (hardships, trials, and tribulations) make him quit doing what he has been chosen to do by the Lord.

His mindset was that he will never give up, he will never quit, and he will finish this because Jesus has told him to do it. When we look over his life, we find out he never quit; he completed his task of leadership. At the end of his apostolic career, the Apostle Paul wrote his final letter from a Roman dungeon to Timothy, his apprentice leader, and says,

"I have fought a good fight, I have finished my course, I have kept the faith: Henceforth there is laid up for me a crown of righteousness which the Lord, the righteous judge, shall give me at that day: and not to me only, but unto all them also that love his appearing." (2 Timothy 4:7 – 8)

He is basically saying I have done everything I could have possibly done. I gave it my best. I have no regrets. I did what Jesus wanted me to do. Therefore, when he examines my life and ministry, he will give me a reward for my service. Wow! What confidence.

He knew he had finished his assignment, and he will receive a crown of righteousness. He knew he would be able to rule with Jesus during the millennial reign (Revelation Ch. 20). His love for Jesus and his desire to reign with Jesus would not let him stop until he finished his assignment.

Here again, I see Paul following in the path of our Lord. The book of Hebrews tells us that Jesus was determined to complete his course too. He wasn't going to stop until he had completed the work the Father had given him to do. The author of Hebrews writes,

"Looking unto Jesus the author and finisher of our faith who for the joy that was set before endured the cross, despising the shame, and is set down at the right hand of the throne of God" (Hebrews 12:2).

The Scripture says that Jesus endured the cross and the shame for what? For the joy that was set before him. What was the joy? It was the joy of sitting at the right hand of the throne of God. He had to finish the work of the cross and its shame to receive the reward the Father had in store for him. Jesus, our Lord, had a goal in mind and an assignment to complete.

What were Jesus's final words on the cross? "It is finished" (John 19:30). His words weren't "It is almost done." Nor "I am about to finish." No, His words were, "It is finished." Everything the Father wanted him to do was finished. His sacrificial work on the cross for sin was finished.

His struggle, pain, and agony were finished. His earthly work and ministry were finished. He finished his course, completed his race, and received his joy and reward. He is currently reigning as he "sits at the right hand of the throne of God." Jesus is a finisher, and his followers must be, too, especially those in church leadership.

Leading With Proper Perspective

༄

If Jesus Christ is the head of the church and hence the source and goal of its entire life, true growth is only possible in obedience to Him. Conversely, if the church becomes detached from Jesus Christ and His Word, it cannot grow however active and successful it may seem to be.

- Os Guinness

When it's all said and done, we must lead with a proper perspective. While the nine disciplines are important and, if practiced, will help us become better leaders. We must remember even with the best leadership, if God the Holy Spirit does not work in the hearts of people, lives will not change, and people will not give their lives to Jesus.

No leader, no matter how talented or intelligent, can make the church produce qualitative (the fruit of the Spirit; Christians acting like Jesus) and quantitative (people becoming Christians through repentance and believing the gospel of Jesus) growth. We must rely on the fact that only Jesus can and will build his church, globally and locally (Matthew 16:18).

It is our job as leaders within his church to accept the privilege, honor, and responsibility of working with him as he builds the church (Mark 16:20). One of the greatest blessings God has given us is his desires to partner with us in ministry. He wants to co-labor with us to help people come to know Jesus and be a part of the process of them become more like him (1 Corinthians 3:9).

Do you remember what God prophesied to Zerubbabel through Zechariah? He said, "Not by might, nor by power, but by my spirit, saith the Lord of host" (Zechariah 4:6). No matter how entrepreneurial and innovative we are, if the Holy Spirit doesn't draw people to Jesus through our efforts, the church will not grow, nor will we have leaders to develop.

We must continually rely on God to do a work in the hearts and minds of people for His glory and for their redemption. Because no matter how many good things we do in our communities, which we must do, "Unless the Lord builds the house, those who build it labor in vain. Unless the Lord watches over the city, the watchman stays awake in vain." (Psalm 127:1, ESV) We must consciously lead with this perspective.

As you read this short book, I pray that you were encouraged and challenged to lead better for Jesus. We all have a long way to go before we can say we are leading like Jesus, but that must be our goal. As we follow in Jesus's leadership footsteps, people will follow in our leadership footsteps. Lives will be changed, and Jesus will be exalted in the earth. Be encouraged and lead. They will follow you as you follow Jesus.

Endnotes

Discipline 9:

1. https://research.lifeway.com/2022/01/05/22-vital-stats-for-ministry-in-2022/
2. https://www.beaconjournal.com/story/news/local/2020/08/22/lsquodifficult-days-are-aheadrsquo-for-americarsquos-churches-faith-institutions/42282593/

Book Recommendations

❦

- *Connect Grow Serve Go* by Bret Robbe and Dwayne McCrary
    - https://www.amazon.com/Connect-Grow-Serve-Go-Balanced/dp/1415867089

- *Christian Beliefs: Twenty Basics Every Christian Should Know* by Wayne Grudem
    - https://www.amazon.com/Christian-Beliefs-Twenty-Basics-Should/dp/0310255996/ref=sr_1_1?crid=35C7KLK5RWLGQ&keywords=20+christian+beliefs&qid=1648065426&sprefix=20+chr%2Caps%2C69&sr=8-1

- *The New One Minute Manager* by Ken Blanchard and Spencer Johnson
    - https://www.amazon.com/The-New-One-Minute-Manager-audiobook/dp/B00UVXZCPO/ref=sr_1_4?crid=WOV2I2C0YROK&keywords=one+minute+manager&qid=1648065505&s=books&sprefix=one+min%2Cstripbooks%2C70&sr=1-4

- *Jesus and The Disinherited* by Howard Thurman
    - https://epiphany-md.org/wp-content/uploads/2019/03/Jesus-and-the-Disinherited-.pdf

- *The Grace of Giving* by John Stott and Chris Wright
    - https://www.amazon.com/Grace-Giving-Gospel-Lausanne-Library-ebook/dp/B07982H7S4

- *The Next Leader* by Stephen Owens
    - https://www.amazon.com/Next-Leader-Stephen-Owens/dp/0982462271/ref=sr_1_1?crid=NUIQADV980E7&keywords=the+next+leaders+stephen+owens&qid=1648067886&s=digital-text&sprefix=the+next+leaders+stephen+owens%2Cdigital-text%2C66&sr=1-1-catcorr

Biography

Stephen Owens is the pastor at Mt. Calvary Baptist Church in Bedford, Ohio. Stephen has over 28 years of ministry experience. He is an author, leadership coach, and church planting trainer.

Stephen has a passion to preach the gospel of Jesus, teach the Bible, and encourage leaders to become all that God wants them to be. Whether they are in the marketplace or in the church, Stephen has an encouraging word for them.

How to contact Stephen:

Amazon Author Center: amazon.com/author/stephenowens1

Email: Owensministry@gmail.com

Website: www.StephenOwens.org www.MtCalvaryofBedford.org

Facebook: https://www.facebook.com/stephen.owens.587

Other books by Stephen:

- The Next Leader
- Dream Chasers

Stephen is available for the following events:

1. Conferences
2. Preaching Engagements
3. Workshops
4. Leadership Coaching

www.ingramcontent.com/pod-product-compliance
Lightning Source LLC
Chambersburg PA
CBHW020700300426
44112CB00007B/467